BEHIND THE SCENES

MANCHESTER UNITED ®

Introduction

All round the world millions of people follow the success of Manchester United on the pitch. Every year some of them, a few hundred thousand, are lucky enough to visit Old Trafford and enjoy a family day out at the heart of United. There they can go on a guided tour of the stadium. They can visit United's brilliant new museum. They can soak up the all-action atmosphere in the club's special video-themed restaurant, the Red Café. And the Old Trafford stores have hundreds of things to buy as reminders of an unforgettable experience. But that still leaves millions of people who never have a chance to discover what makes Old Trafford so special.

ntroduction • In

Behind the Scenes 3

Introduction

Old Trafford Behind The Scenes takes you round United's famous stadium describing the bits you see on television and lots of fascinating areas away from the pitch and the terraces.

Introduction • In

Open the pages that follow and find out for yourself why the museum has the stuffed head of a famous goat in its collection, what it's like in United's dressing room, what tasty thing in the Red Café do Phil Neville and his family really like and what it's like to be a United mascot on match day.

If you ever wanted to know what it's like behind the scenes at the world's greatest football club – the answer is in your hands. Look inside and find out for yourself.

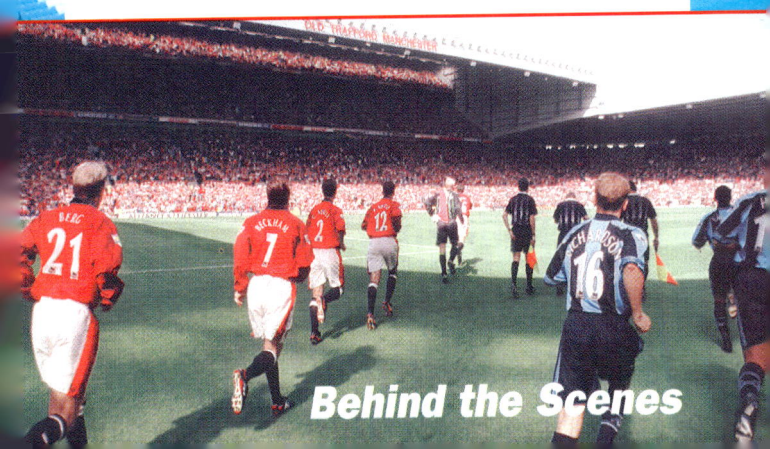

Behind the Scenes

Around the S...

Sir Bobby Charlton gave Old Trafford its other famous name, The Theatre of Dreams, and United's great stadium holds its special magic even for the people who see it every day of their working lives. When Alex Ferguson was asked recently what he felt about it, he described the excitement he still gets whenever he walks into the stadium – especially when it's empty. If he wasn't the manager, he thought the next best job would be to be a tour guide, spending his day talking to people about something he holds so dear to his heart.

Even though Old Trafford is by far the biggest football stadium in the English Premiership, it could still be filled for every game even if it was twice the size.

Old Trafford

adium • Around

That's how great the support is for Manchester United. Every match is all-ticket and every game is sold out.

The club is always looking at ways of improving the stadium and during the 1995 – 96 season the new North Stand was opened in stages. When the last section opened on 17 April 1996, this one stand was able to hold 25,100 spectators. That's more than some whole grounds of other Premiership clubs can hold!

Behind the Scenes 7

Around the St

The builders used 4,000 tonnes of steel and 4,500 tonnes of concrete to build the huge three-tier stand. The roof is the largest roof of its type in Europe – it's a cantilevered roof, which means it's fixed at the back and then reaches out over the seats without needing any supports at the front. It's so big in fact that the Old Trafford pitch could fit on top of it!

Old Trafford

adium • Around

The lowest tier of seats in the North Stand has coloured seats spelling out MANCHESTER UNITED. There are 1,316 white seats and 479 black seats used in these sixteen letters. Almost as many white seats are used in the East Stand where 1,312 white seats spell out the name UMBRO and form the logo of the club's official kit sponsor.

Opposite the North Stand is a platform hanging below the roof of the South Stand. This is the television gantry where the TV cameras are placed. They get a brilliant view of the game from up there, but it isn't always as good as it sounds. You need a good head for heights. Up on the gantry they're 12m above the pitch and in winter it can get very, very cold. But even that is nothing compared with the television

Behind the Scenes

camera operators who are lifted up over the roof of the stadium on a massive extending arm to get a bird's-eye view of the pitch. They get lifted to a height of 65m above the ground!

Down in the lower corner of the South Stand and the Scoreboard End the club has created a special platform where disabled spectators and spectators who are blind or can't see very well can enjoy the match.

This platform has seventy places for wheelchairs and seventy seats for those who bring the people in wheelchairs to the stadium. Behind these places are special seats for the spectators who have problems with their sight. Each of them can listen to a live description of the match on headphones. This is the same match commentary that Manchester United

adium • Around

Behind the Scenes 11

broadcasts to local hospitals. In this way the club makes it possible for its disabled spectators to enjoy the excitement and add their voices to the special Old Trafford atmosphere.

Better still – the club provides all this for free!

Above this special section of the stand there are 3,000 seats which are usually reserved for visiting supporters, when United are playing at home in the Premiership. Visiting clubs can have more tickets for FA Cup matches. So United usually let them sit in the Scoreboard End instead.

adium • Around

Behind the Scenes 13

Around the S

When the scoreboard was installed in Old Trafford in 1973 it was one of the first electronic scoreboards in the country. Since then it has recorded many memorable victories, but few will ever beat the score that clicked up on 4 March 1995. That showed UNITED 9–0 IPSWICH. It was the highest ever score achieved in a Premier League match!

On the far side of the stadium, in the corner between the Stretford End and the South Stand are the 4,200 seats of the club's Family Stand. Only parents and children are allowed to sit here and it's the only part of the ground where United's supporters and visiting supporters sit together.

Old Trafford

adium•Around

That's to encourage young supporters from different clubs to mix in a friendly way. It's also the only part of the stadium where smoking is not allowed. Underneath the seats in the Family Stand there's an entertainment area where the club provides all sorts things from face painting to a magician to amuse kids on match days.

Behind the Scenes 15

Around the St

The first time you walk into Old Trafford to watch a night-time match your attention is grabbed by the dazzling ring of light all round the stadium. This comes from the floodlights mounted on the roofs of the stands – 118 of them fitted with long-life

Old Trafford

dium • Around

lamps that can last up to two seasons. Under these lights Old Trafford looks like a huge theatre with a glorious green stage. Bobby Charlton was so right – it really is the Theatre of Dreams.

Behind the Scenes

Private Boxes

Manchester United is so often the first club to try new football ideas. In 1966 United opened the first **private box** at Old Trafford – the first in any football ground. At that time a lot of people thought it was a strange idea. Who would want to watch any football match, not to mention a United home game, from behind a glass screen? But United knew better and thirty years later Old Trafford has 181 private boxes, many more than any other football club – and the waiting list for them keeps on growing!

The boxes are arranged in a ring around the stadium. The North Stand has the 32 newest boxes. Sixteen of these seat six people and the other sixteen seat eight people.

Old Trafford

Private Boxes

Behind the Scenes

Private Boxes

The rest of the private boxes vary in size with seating for five to eight people. Each box has a volume control knob that turns up or down the level of noise from the stadium outside. There's also a television set, so that the spectators in the box can watch immediate action replays – and so can the fans in the four of five rows of seats outside, if they turn round!

There's also waiter service to supply refreshments during the game. If you want to watch football in luxury – this is the way to do it as thousands of people discover every season.

Old Trafford

Private Boxes

Behind the Scenes 21

The Centre Tunnel

The Centre Tunnel at Old Trafford may not look the most exciting part of this famous stadium but it carries its own importance, because it's the oldest part. The Centre Tunnel is all that remains of the original stadium that opened at Old Trafford in 1910. During the Second World War two-thirds of the stadium was destroyed in an enemy bombing raid on 11 March 1941.

While rebuilding work took place after the war had ended, United were invited by Manchester City to share their ground at Maine Road. However, the builders at Old Trafford found that the Centre Tunnel had survived the air raid. Its thick concrete walls had not

nel • The Centr

been damaged by the exploding bombs, so it was left intact while the rest of the stadium was rebuilt.

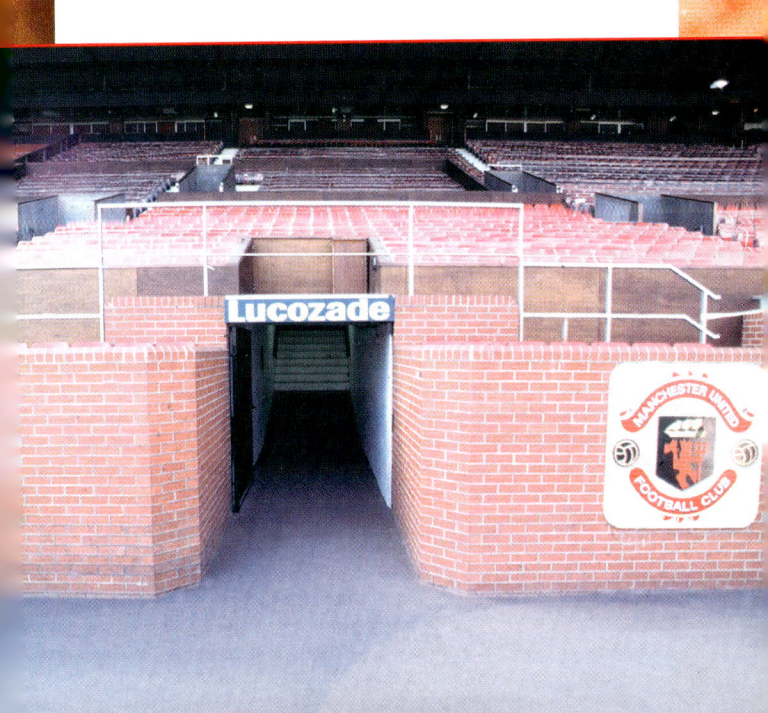

The Centre Tu...

The tunnel was still in use until quite recently. Since the players stopped using it steps have been built down it. But when it was in use it was the steepest sloping tunnel in the English Football League, which may explain why the players always ran out onto the pitch the way they did!

Nowadays the Centre Tunnel can still be the focus of attention during matches, because immediately above it is the bench where Alex Ferguson sits during a match with Brian Kidd, David Fevre the physio and the subs. The manager prefers this position to the old dugouts because it provides a better view of the game.

nnel • The Cent

Behind the Scenes 25

The Pitch

The Old Trafford pitch is one of the top playing surfaces in the Premiership, in fact it was voted the best of all in 1995. Until the summer of 1998 there was a camber on the pitch – the surface was slightly curved. The centre spot was some 23cm higher than the touchlines and bylines. People sitting in the front row of seats could sometimes see players' legs disappearing from view on the other side of the pitch! But the camber served a very important purpose. It helped the pitch drain well. Today, modern technology has taken over and there is no longer a need for such a big camber. That's why the Old Trafford pitch was flattened and lowered in the summer of 1998 leaving it with only a very slight camber.

Pitch•The Pitc

The Pitch

This was also the occasion when for the first time ever fans were able to take a piece of the pitch home with them. When it was lifted the turf was cut into 10,000 pieces and, over two days in the middle of May, 10,000 lucky museum visitors went to Old Trafford to collect a piece of the pitch which became theirs to keep for ever. Cutting the grass at home must have taken on a new interest after that!

The Old Trafford turf is grown from four different varieties of hard-wearing grass seed. Today it comes delivered to the stadium, ready for use, in huge trays measuring over a metre square and 10cm deep. This makes it possible to replace quite large areas of the playing surface between matches.

Pitch•The Pitc

The Pitch

Keeping the turf in tip-tip condition requires a lot of experience and careful stadium design. The roofs of the South Stand and Stretford End are fitted with huge translucent panels, which let sunlight shine through to the pitch to help the grass grow thick and healthy. Old Trafford also has its own water supply. There are three underground springs flowing beneath the stadium which give a regular supply of water. In addition 85 per cent of rain-water that falls on the pitch drains into a massive 245,000-litre tank under the East Stand. So almost every drop of water is recycled. Around the ground is a computer-controlled sprinkler system which can squirt out 250 litres of water per minute onto the turf.

Another secret of the Old Trafford playing surface lies some 25cm below the surface. There, around 37km of plastic pipe snake backwards and forwards the full length of the pitch to provide an under-soil heating system. This works just like a central heating system at home, only on a massive scale! At Old Trafford there's a huge gas-fired boiler that heats the water which is pumped through the pipe network below

The Pitch

the pitch to defrost the pitch, or even melt snow. Thanks to this it is very unlikely that a match ever has to be cancelled because of bad weather.

Another reason for the pitch being kept in such good condition is that the club is very strict about who is allowed to walk on it. Visitors on tours see signs asking them not to walk on the grass and the tour guides ask them not to as well. Even the people who work for Manchester United do not walk on the pitch without permission. In this way the playing surface has as little wear and tear as possible.

Pitch • The Pi

The Ticket Office

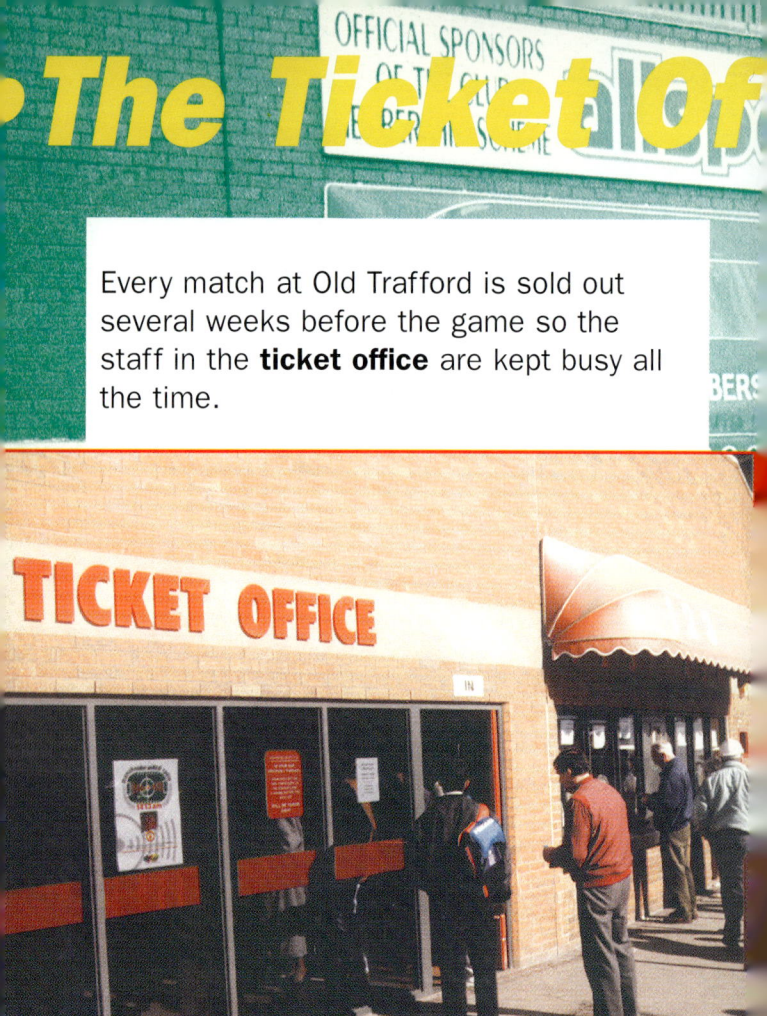

Every match at Old Trafford is sold out several weeks before the game so the staff in the **ticket office** are kept busy all the time.

34 *Old Trafford*

They have to deal with ticket enquiries from all over the world because Manchester United has official supporters-clubs right round the globe from New South Wales in Australia to New York State in the USA. Visitors often ask tour guides about the club's worldwide support.

One guide was asked if there was anywhere that didn't have a Manchester United supporter. The guide was just about to answer when he was interrupted by the loud speakers round the stadium announcing *'Would the representative from Mars please go to reception!'* The timing couldn't have been better.

The Ticket Of

To be fair to all its supporters, the club carefully controls the number of season tickets it sells. This is limited to 34,750 season tickets. Even having £1,000,000 pounds can't buy you a season ticket at Old Trafford once they've all been sold. This was proved when a supporter won £1,000,000 or more on the National Lottery. One of the things he wanted most was a Manchester

36 Old Trafford

ce • The Ticket

United season ticket, but sadly no more were available that year and he had to wait with all the other people hoping to get one for the following season.

MANCHESTER UTD. F.C. LTD.
OLD TRAFFORD • MANCHESTER
EUROPEAN CHAMPIONS CLUB CUP
SEMI-FINAL — 1st LEG

MANCHESTER UNITED
v
REAL MADRID
(SPAIN)

WED., 24th APRIL
Kick-off 7-45 p.m.

Admission 10/-

Olive
Secretary

Issued subject to the Rules, Regulations and Bye-Laws of the Football Association.
Ticket exchanged nor money refunded.

Portion To Be Retained

PADDOCK
UNITED ROAD
ADULTS
Enter by turnstiles
21—29, 34

Nº 5844

As a capacity attendance is expected, it is strongly recommended that patrons ENTER THE GROUND not less than 30 minutes before kick-off.

Behind the Scenes **37**

The Stadium

Visitors to Old Trafford are always very impressed by the **Stadium Control Room**. As its name suggests, this is the engine room of the club on a match day. It's the room where club officials work alongside police officers to make sure everything runs smoothly, before, during and after a game.

From the **Stadium Control Room** the police and officials on duty have an unbeatable view all round Old Trafford, thanks to 27 television monitors linked to almost as many cameras inside and outside the ground.

One of the police officers on duty also acts a 'spotter', scanning the ground through a pair of high-density binoculars on the look-out for any trouble spots in the crowd. If he or she does spot any problem the operators of the cameras inside the stadium can zoom in to get a close-up view of what is going on. The

ontrol Room

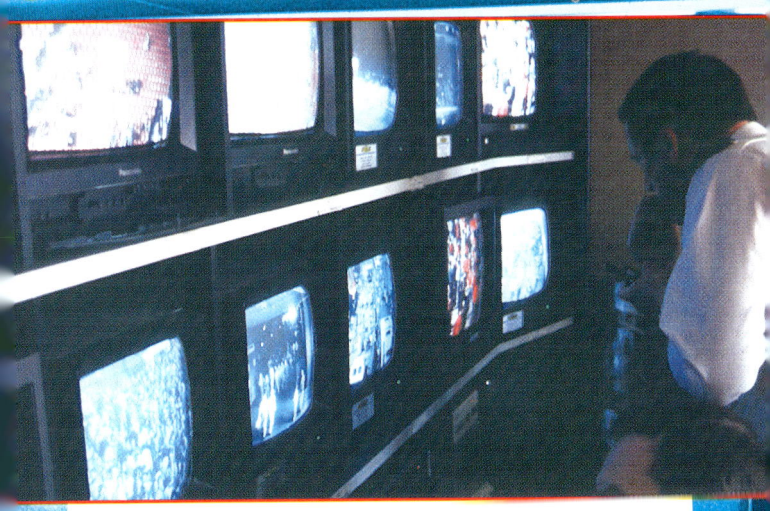

cameras are so powerful that even at the furthest point of the ground it is possible to get a good picture of just one person in the crowd of over 55,000. On one occasion a sharp-eyed police officer even spotted an escaped convict in the new North Stand! As all the cameras are linked to printers the police can print a picture if they think it might be useful for their enquiries.

Behind the Scenes

The Stadium

Crowd safety is always the top concern on match days and Old Trafford has a 'turnstile control unit' operated by a computer in the Stadium Control Room. This keeps a record of the number of spectators who enter the different parts of the stadium. As soon as the right number of people have passed through a turnstile, the computer automatically closes it. In that way there is no danger of more people entering the stadium than should be allowed.

Another important safety feature is the central control that operates all fifty-five exit gates. If the official on duty pushes a button in the Stadium Control Room, all the gates will open to let the spectators leave the stadium. Using this system the whole of Old Trafford can be emptied in under twelve minutes!

ontrol Room

There are also special gates that allow spectators to move onto the pitch to safety. The head groundsman would not be too pleased about this of course, but in a club where safety comes first every care is taken to look after everyone coming to a match – and just to make sure that it's working, the Stadium Control Room operators test every piece of their high-tech safety equipment in the ground on match days before spectators are allowed inside.

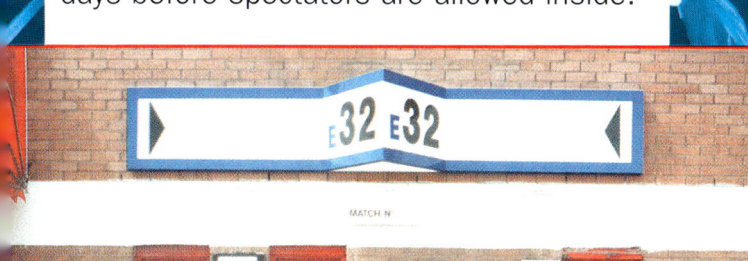

The Players'

The Players' Lounge is where the players come before and after a game on match day – that's the only time they use it. When United are playing at home, the players always arrive at the stadium about three hours before kick-off. And the first thing they do is to sit down to a carefully prepared pre-match meal in one of the Old Trafford restaurants.

When the meal's finished they go to the Players' Lounge to relax before crossing the corridor to the dressing room to change for the match and meet the manager. Players' wives and children use the lounge as well and while the game is being played two nannies look after the players' younger children in a specially fitted-out crèche next to the Players' Lounge.

Old Trafford

ounge•The Pla

Behind the 43

The Players'

After the game the Manchester United captain invites the visiting team into the lounge for a drink and a chat before they set off home. Even the United manager usually needs an invitation before entering the Players' Lounge, though he has two lounges of his own where he can entertain his guests on a match day.

One wall in the Players' Lounge carries the international Honours Board which names every player who has won at least one international cap whilst playing for Manchester United. All round the room are photographs of several of these players along with other famous faces. These are the captains of Manchester United since the Second World War.

ounge • The Pla

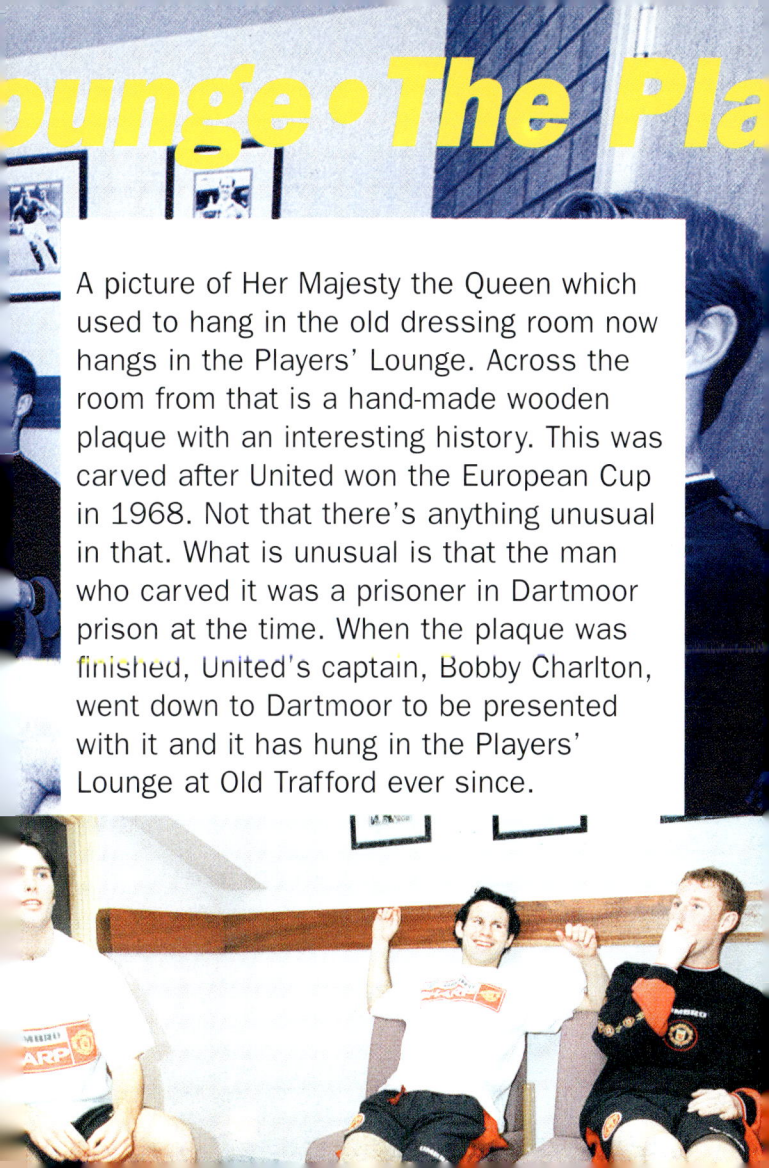

A picture of Her Majesty the Queen which used to hang in the old dressing room now hangs in the Players' Lounge. Across the room from that is a hand-made wooden plaque with an interesting history. This was carved after United won the European Cup in 1968. Not that there's anything unusual in that. What is unusual is that the man who carved it was a prisoner in Dartmoor prison at the time. When the plaque was finished, United's captain, Bobby Charlton, went down to Dartmoor to be presented with it and it has hung in the Players' Lounge at Old Trafford ever since.

The one place every visitor to Old Trafford wants to see is **United's team dressing room** and who can blame them! If the walls could speak, imagine the stories they could tell of famous wins, incredible goals and all the triumphs the team has had in its proud history.

All the tour guides will tell you that the dressing room is the high point of the tour of Old Trafford. Like every other home dressing room in the country United's has features that aren't found in the visitors' dressing room. There's a colour television for the players to look at if they want to find out the results of other matches being played at the same time, or if they want to listen to what the television commentators are saying about them!

ressing Room

The United dressing room also has two tactics boards on which the manager and players plot their plan for the game. You won't find tactics boards in the visitors' dressing room – United don't want to encourage their opponents to plot tactics against them.

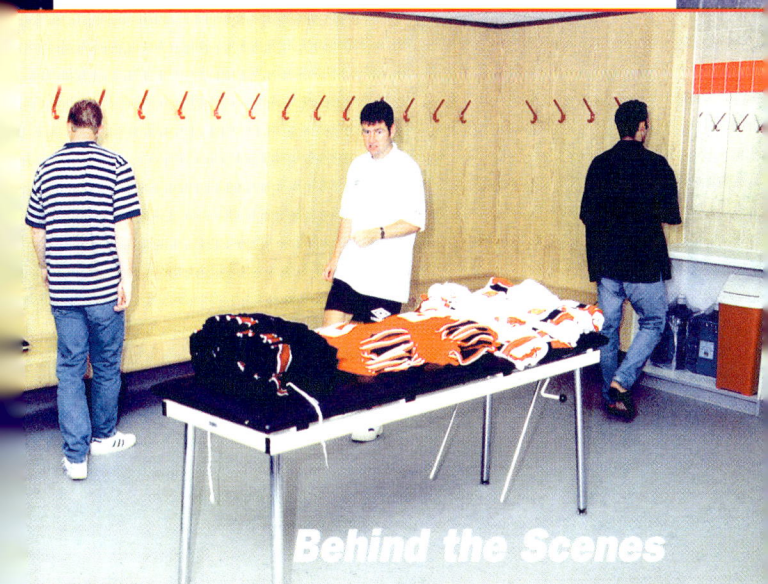

Behind the Scenes

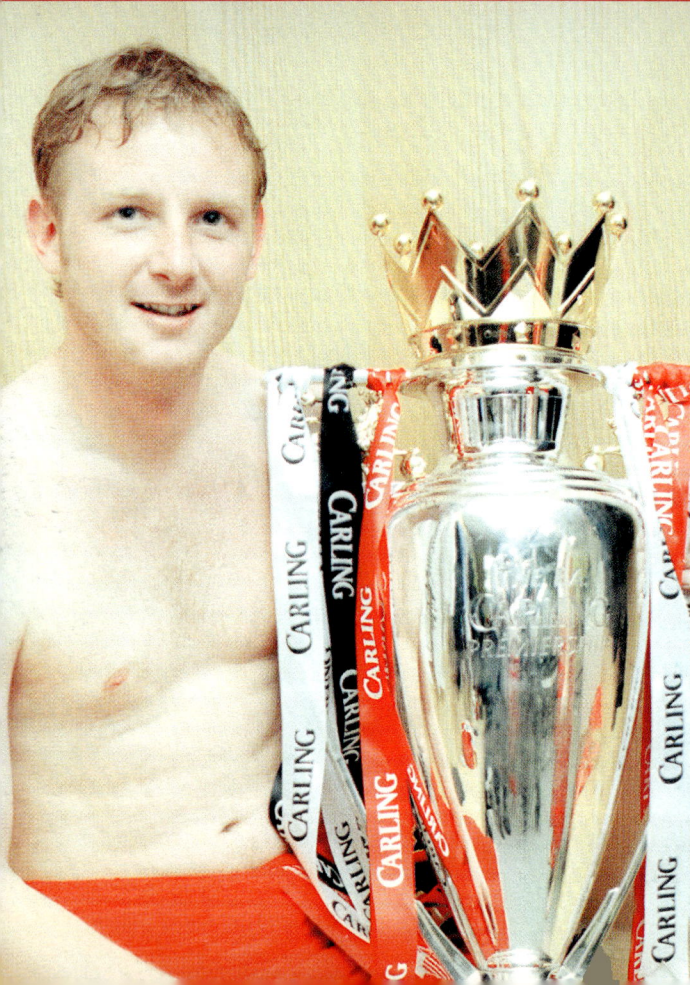

The Players'

ressing Room

A third extra made available to the United players is a room measuring about four metres square and fitted with an Astroturf floor. Apart from this special flooring the room is completely empty, because this is the United warm-up room where the players can go to do their warm-up exercises once they're ready and changed for the match.

When the game is over the United players can relax in the big bath, a giant spa pool filled with bubbling water in which six players can bathe at a time. After playing at home, United's players can enjoy a good soak with their mates as they talk over the game.

The United dressing room is big enough for eighteen players. It has to accommodate this number for European Championship games. The Kit Manager is very precise in the way he lays out the team strips for them before a game. He starts in one corner of the dressing room with Peter Schmeichel's kit (no 1) and works his way round, laying out the kit for the other players in numerical order, except for no 13, Brian McClair. Brian is the senior professional at Manchester United and he likes to have his kit on the bench between numbers 3 and 4. Thanks to this precise order, the tour guides can inform visitors of exactly where their favourite players sit and get changed.

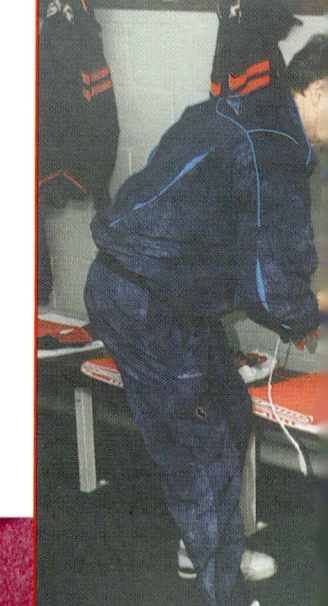

50 Old Trafford

… ressing Room …

Peter Schmeichel follows his own routine after the pre-match meal. As goalkeeper he likes to focus his mind by going straight into the dressing room to relax on a physio treatment bench reading the paper or watching television.

The Players'

Alongside the clean lines of the bench and the sparkling white tiles of the washing area, the United dressing room has one unexpected piece of furniture. This is a beautifully carved tall wooden chair that tells the story of Alex Ferguson. The chair was made by a friend of the manager's and at its top are the carved words 'Oor Fergie'. Down the chair are carvings of symbols from the coat of arms of Glasgow, his home city: among them birds, a bell, a fish and a tree. There are five thistles representing Alex, his wife and their three sons. There's another thistle, a knotted one, which represents Scottish marriage and the seat of the chair is formed in the shape of a Catherine wheel which represents the manager's wife, whose name is also Catherine. Either side of the chair are brass fittings from Alex Ferguson's old school. And inside the legs on both sides is carved the name Matt, after Sir Matt Busby, who Alex Ferguson respects so highly as a football manager. This chair is a marvellous tribute to friendship and the best spirit of football.

The Players'

It's a sign of the same strong spirit within the club that when the referee rings the bell to call the teams out onto the pitch, Alex Ferguson and his players all shake hands in the dressing room and wish each

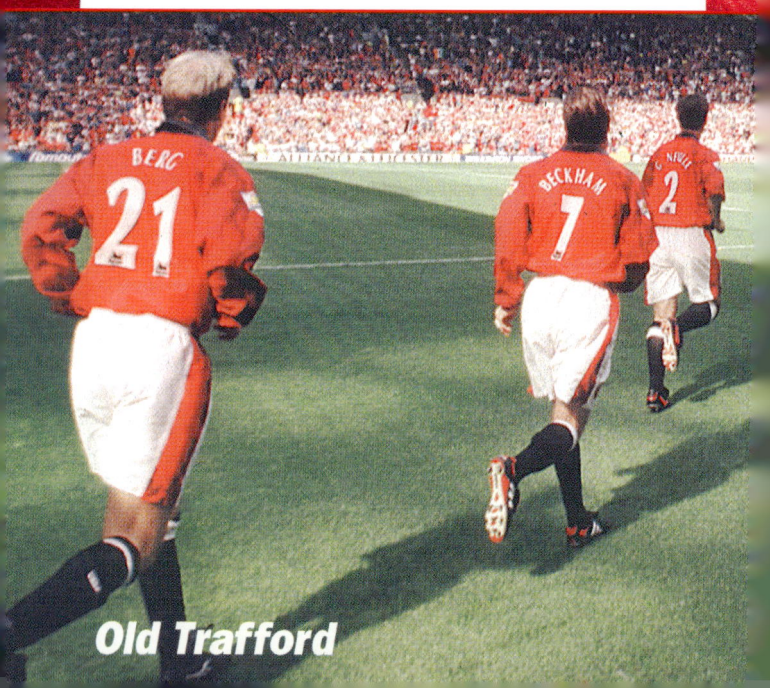

Old Trafford

ressing Room

other good luck. Then they file out down the Players' Tunnel to be met by the roar from over 55,000 spectators cheering them as they run onto the pitch.

Behind the Scenes

The Mascots

FEELING FAMOUS FOR A DAY – MANCHESTER UNITED'S MASCOTS

Can you imagine what it must be like to walk down the Players' Tunnel and out onto the pitch at Old Trafford for a home game? Think what it must sound like to hear 55,000 people cheering when they see you. Think what it must feel like to look up into the new North Stand and see 25,000 people waving and clapping when you jog out.

Of course, the Manchester United players know the thrill they get every time they run onto the pitch in the Theatre of Dreams – but they aren't the only ones to discover what it's like. For most home games specially selected boys and girls get the chance to share this excitement. They're the mascots, dressed in the United strip, who come out with the team at the start of the match.

The Mascots • T

Two members of the club staff look after the mascots and their families while they're at Old Trafford. The mascots arrive in good time before the match. About an hour-and-a-half before kick-off they go down to the dressing-room area, to get changed in the Ball Boys dressing room. Once they're ready, the mascots and their families watch the players run out to warm up and sometimes the mascots can get an autograph or two, even a photograph, as the players return to the dressing room.

When the referee rings the bell to call the players on to the pitch for the match, the mascots wait for the team at the top of the tunnel and the United captain usually goes out with them. That's when the mums and dads take the all-important photographs of their kids running out with their favourite team.

Out on the pitch, the mascots kick the ball about with the players for a minute or two. Then they go to the centre circle to see the referee toss the coin. Some referees give the mascots Premier League badges to keep as a souvenir.

he Mascots • T

Some give them the 50p coins they've tossed to start the games. One little girl even had the chance to toss the coin herself!

Behind the Scenes 59

The Mascots

There's time for one last picture with the referee and his officials, and the two captains. That's taken by the club's official photographer, then the mascot looks up to see Fred The Red dancing on the touch-line, showing where he or she has to run off so that the game can begin. Phew!

Back with their families and the club staff, the mascot quickly gets changed and then rounds off an unforgettable day by going into the stadium to watch the game.

he Mascots • T

Behind the Scenes *61*

The Players'

Next to the Family Stand is the **Players' Tunnel**, which took over from the old Centre Tunnel when work on the Stretford End was completed in 1993. The corridor from the dressing rooms leads into the tunnel and this is where United and the visiting team line up side by side before they run out on to the pitch.

The name, **Players' Tunnel**, only tells half of the story of this important part of Old Trafford, because it's also a roadway right onto the pitch from outside the stadium. The roof of the tunnel can be lifted 7.6m, so that ambulances, fire engines and other tall vehicles can drive into the ground. This is necessary if the club needs to set up huge television screens to show important away games, or if special equipment is needed for some of the other events that take place in the stadium. International rugby matches have been staged at Old Trafford. Boxing matches have been fought here. There have been pop concerts and the television programme *Songs of Praise* was broadcast from United's ground when spectators from many different clubs came together to sing hymns and pray in this

The Players'

popular programme which is shown on Sunday evenings.

At the opposite end of the **Players' Tunnel**, the end nearest the outside of the stadium, there are huge gates that can be opened to let visiting team coaches drive right into the tunnel.

When the time comes for the teams to come onto the pitch, they run down the tunnel and through a white plastic cover which can be pulled out close to the edge of the playing area. This is designed to protect the players while they're running out. When they're on the pitch ready to start the game, the expanding cover is pushed back out of the way.

nnel • The Play

Press Lounge

The Press Lounge and Auditorium is where all the newspaper reporters covering the match gather. At Old Trafford the auditorium looks like a small theatre. It's got sixty comfortable chairs where the reporters sit looking at a raised desk with a smart wooden front and microphones. It's here that Alex Ferguson comes after every home match to hold a press conference and answer questions, usually with one of the United players he'll have brought with him. After he's finished the manager of the visiting team will come in to give his press conference with one of his players.

The room is also used for press conferences on other subjects. Players sometimes sign for the club in front of the press in the auditorium – Andy Cole was

nd Auditorium

just one of the many stars to sign here when he joined United.

Manchester United are very careful to make sure that everything to do with the club has the same top-quality feel about it. Manchester United wants to be seen as the best at everything it does.

Shopping at O...

Anyone who visits the **Megastore**, the **Superstore** and the **Matchday store**, or buys anything from the catalogue, can see this for themselves. Unfortunately the official things that Manchester United sells have been so popular that some people try to copy them and steal business from the club by selling fakes and cheap imitations. The club is always on the look-out for people making cheap replica kit and faking other things it sells, so that the police can arrest them and the courts can punish them.

When you buy anything officially approved by the club there's no doubt that you're buying the best – that's what you want after all. So does everyone else, including the players, who go shopping in the stores with their families and friends for replica

'd Trafford • Sh

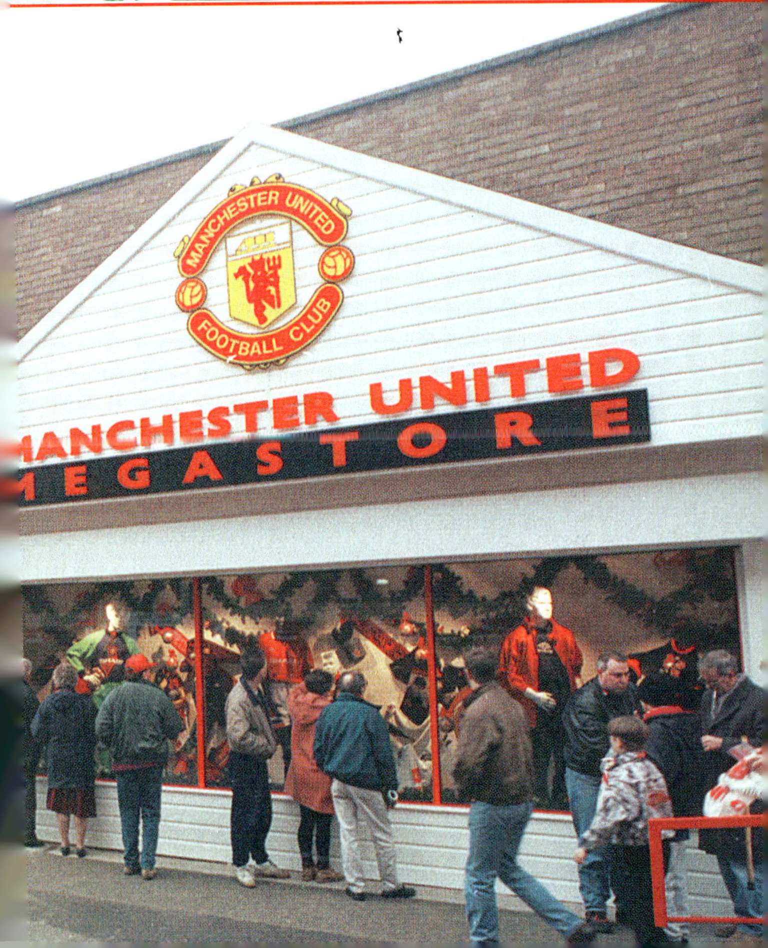

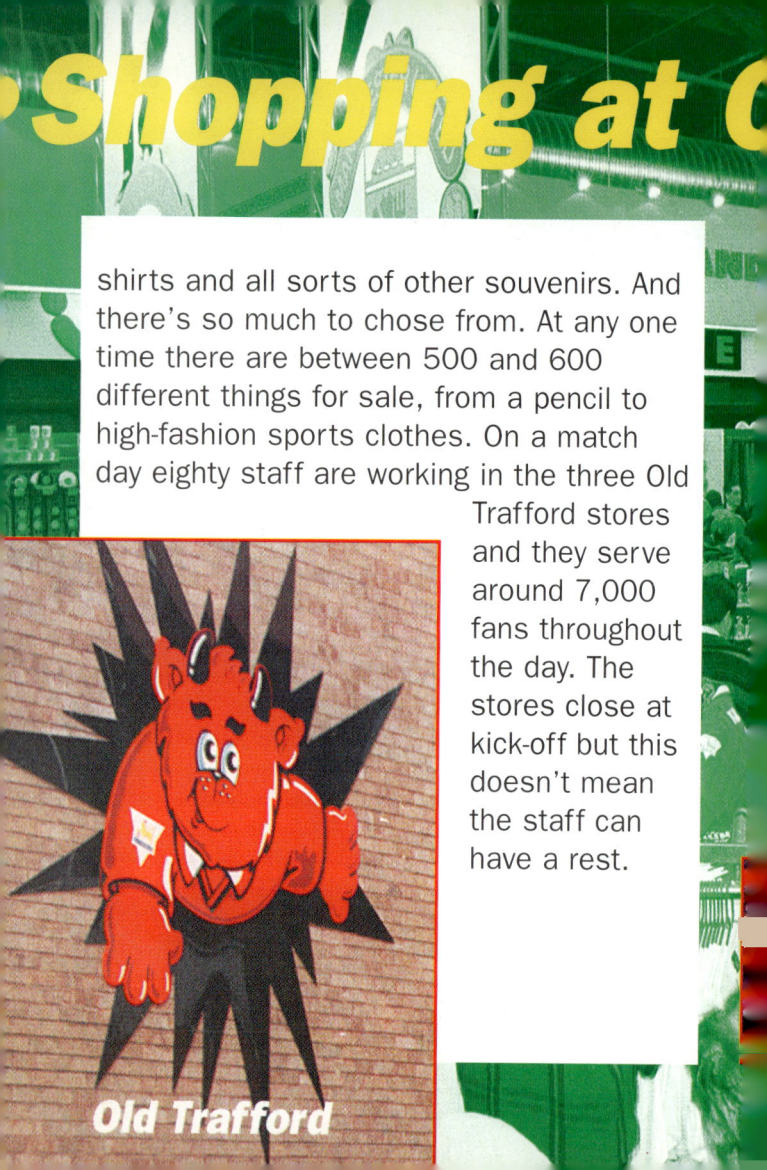

Shopping at O...

shirts and all sorts of other souvenirs. And there's so much to chose from. At any one time there are between 500 and 600 different things for sale, from a pencil to high-fashion sports clothes. On a match day eighty staff are working in the three Old Trafford stores and they serve around 7,000 fans throughout the day. The stores close at kick-off but this doesn't mean the staff can have a rest.

Old Trafford

d Trafford • Sh

Behind the Scenes 71

Shopping at O

They have to restock and price replacements for all the things that have been sold, so that they are ready for

Old Trafford

ld Trafford•Sh

business again fifteen minutes before the final whistle. Like everything else at Old Trafford, it's all go on match days!

Behind the Scenes

The Museum

Manchester United scored another first in May 1986 when the club opened Britain's very first **museum** devoted to football. In its second year 26,137 people visited the Museum and Tour Centre at Old Trafford. By the end of 1996 just under 200,000 people were passing through the doors every year. United's past history was proving to be just as popular as the club's present-day success. The time had come for this exciting Old Trafford feature to grow and in April 1998 a brand new museum, filled with new ideas, new things to see and new things to do, opened on three floors of the massive North Stand.

The Museum•T

Behind the Scenes 75

The Museum

The club spent £4,000,000 in creating a state-of-the-art attraction to take United forward into the 21st century. Among the traditional showcase displays visitors can trace the club's history back to 1878, when it first started under the name of Newton Heath Lancashire and Yorkshire Railway Cricket and Football Club. You can see how the kit has changed from the days when badges were only used in cup finals, to the modern high-tech kit worn on and off the field today.

Look out too for a goat's head hanging in pride of place. This is Billy the goat, Manchester United's lucky mascot when they won the FA Cup in 1909.

The Museum

That was the first time United had won the cup and there was great rejoicing. In Billy's case the rejoicing was a bit too great and he never recovered from the celebrations.

Behind the Scenes

The Museum

However, after he died United were not going to forget the good luck Billy had brought them and his stuffed head is a reminder of triumphs the club went on to throughout the rest of the 20th century. A panel of experts has selected fifteen players from United's history who feature in the special Hall of Fame and many of them have loaned the museum their personal medals and kit that can be seen on display.

Every single player who has ever played for the United first team is included in the huge database that the museum staff have put together.

Old Trafford

The Museum

Around the museum are twenty interactive computer monitors which flash up information about players and information

The Museum

about matches (including television highlights), so you can find out all you ever wanted to know about hundreds of players and games right back to the earliest days of the club – and all at the touch of a button. The same interactive system has quizzes to test your knowledge about the club or takes you on a virtual reality tour of Old Trafford.

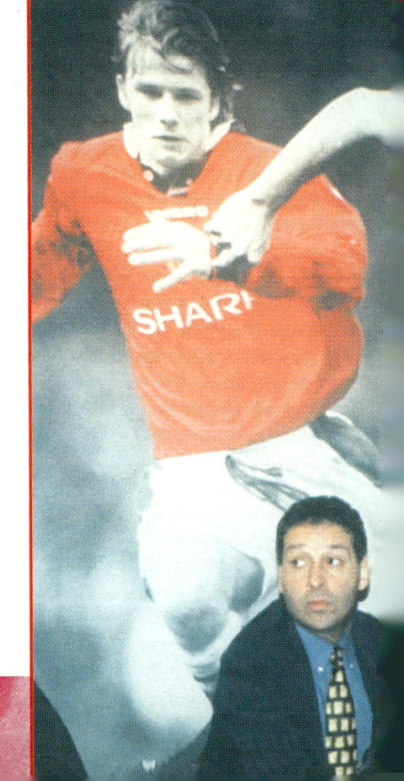

The Museum • T

The Museum

The United Museum was opened in April 1998 by the greatest footballer in the history of the game and 'Sportsman of the Century', the Brazilian star player Pelé. To mark this historic event the museum staged an exhibition to celebrate his amazing career, which included three World Cup wins. Pelé lent many of his personal football treasures to this exhibition, which shows the respect he must have for England's top football club.

Old Trafford

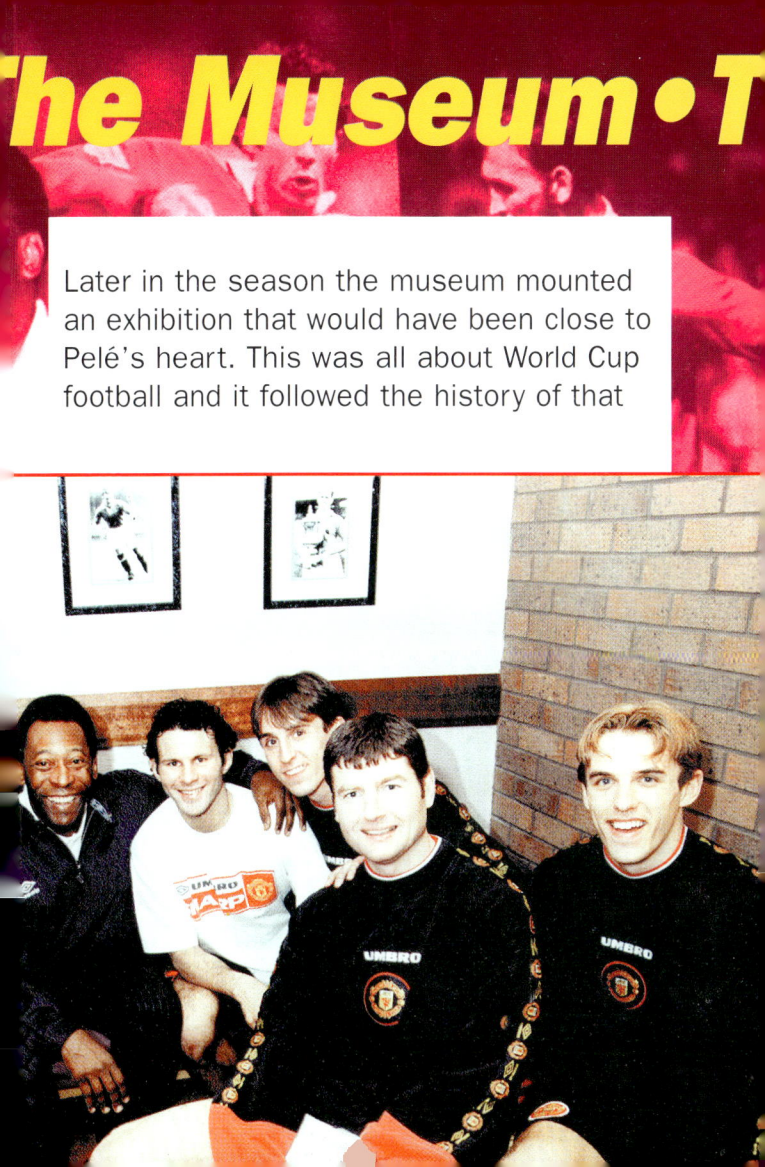

The Museum • T

Later in the season the museum mounted an exhibition that would have been close to Pelé's heart. This was all about World Cup football and it followed the history of that

The Museum

great competition from the first World Cup tournament in Uruguay in 1930 right up to the Manchester United players who were in action in World Cup '98. The same museum space will have other special interest exhibitions in the years ahead.

The Museum • T

And in case anyone needs reminding just how successful Manchester United have been over the years, a visit to the museum's Trophy Room will show the glittering success the club's teams have had, from the European Cup to the Premier League.

The Museum

Like any serious museum, Manchester United's has space for people to study the club's history using books, match programmes, newspaper cuttings and photographs. There's a special area set aside for visiting school and college parties and you can imagine how many kids and students jump at the chance to go to Old Trafford! In 1997 alone there were 400 educational visits by school and college groups.

You could fill a book about the museum itself – the only answer is to visit it. No true Red will be able to keep away!

86 Old Trafford

The Museum •

Another Side

You'd expect a club as successful as Manchester United on the football field to take the same success into all the other things it does.

There's the brilliant new museum crammed with exciting new displays. There are the fabulous stores filled with all the Manchester United goodies you ever dreamed of. There's the Red Café, of course (more about that in a moment). But there's something else – something that keeps Old Trafford humming with activity all through the year even when there isn't a spectator in the stadium or a player on the pitch. Any ideas?

Old Trafford

It's a special business all of its own that the club's developed and it's based round the Manchester United Executive Suites. These are eleven impressive rooms in the heart of Old Trafford which the club lets people hire for events such as meetings, exhibitions, parties, weddings, right up to huge business functions to which 1,000 people might be invited. Can you think of anywhere better to hold a big occasion? Not many people can, and this side of the Manchester United business is making the club as popular behind the terraces as it is down on the pitch.

Behind the Scenes

Food, Gloriou...

With such a lot of important events taking place in the Manchester United Executive Suites, the club has a team of chefs who prepare food for every sort of occasion. On top of this the club runs the Stretford restaurant, overlooking the pitch, which serves lunch from Tuesday to Friday, as well as its famous Red Café.

The Red Café is United's own official themed video restaurant in the back of the North Stand, just across from the Museum. Walk in and you come face to face with a video wall showing non-stop United action you won't see anywhere else, because the videos played in the Red Café are specially put together for the Red Café.

Food •Food,

Food, Glorious

Two hundred people at a time can sit down here to enjoy a cup of coffee, a light snack or delicious dinner. Sometimes visitors are lucky enough to catch sight of players coming in for a bite to eat. The **Red Café** banana splits were a great hit with David Beckham and the Neville family are huge fans of the Red Café's own red sauce – and not just because there's a picture of Phil Neville on the label! The sauce is delicious and it's specially made for Manchester United. You can't get it anywhere else. As the label says, anything else is just ketchup.

To look after all these hungry people Manchester United employs about 150 full-time staff in its catering department. On a match day that number swells to 1,000. And on a match day a lot of people want to eat at Old Trafford! Five thousand hot meals are

Food • Food,

prepared in the restaurants and dining-rooms. Then there are the 39 kiosks around the ground which provide food to the spectators on the terraces: 10,000 Manchester United pies are served at an average home match, along with 11,000 litres of cola, tea and coffee.

Food, Glorious

Even after food and drink has been served to these tens of thousands of people on a match day, the club's cleaning staff can still make ready an executive suite for a special function only a few hours later. So United could play at home, with 55,000 people filling Old Trafford in the afternoon to watch them, and in the evening a special occasion can be celebrated somewhere in the stadium that looks as smart and welcoming as a top-class hotel.

It's being able to do things like that which keeps Manchester United special – behind the scenes as well on the football field.

Food • Food,

First published in 1998 by Manchester United Books, an imprint of
VCI, 76 Dean Street, London, W1V 5HA.
Web site: www.vci.co.uk.

Text copyright © 1998 Manchester United Books

The right of Clive Dickinson to be identified as the author of this work has been asserted by him in accordance with the Copyright, Designs and Patents Act 1998

10 9 8 7 6 5 4 3 2 1

All rights reserved. This book is sold subject to the condition that it may not be reproduced, stored in a retrieval system, or transmitted, in any form or by any means, electronic, mechanical, photocopying, recording or otherwise, without the publisher's prior consent.

A catalogue record for this title is available from the British Library

ISBN 0 233 99371 1
Designed by Words & Pictures Ltd
Printed in Italy

Photographs by John Peters, Action Images, Allsport, Empics and Popperfoto

With special thanks to John Peters, Rachel Jervis, Cliff Butler and Mike Laganis at Manchester United.